W9-APS-271

WHO LIVES HERE?

RAIN FORESTS

Mary-Jane Wilkins

BROWN BEAR BOOKS

Published by Brown Bear Books Ltd

4877 N. Circulo Bujia
Tucson, AZ 85718
USA

and

First Floor
9–17 St Albans Place
London N1 0NX

© 2017 Brown Bear Books Ltd

ISBN 978-1-78121-349-0

Library of Congress Cataloging-in-Publication Data available on request

Picture Researcher: Clare Newman
Designer: Melissa Roskell
Design Manager: Keith Davis
Editorial Director: Lindsey Lowe
Children's Publisher: Anne O'Daly

Printed in China

Picture Credits

The photographs in this book are used by permission and through the courtesy of:

Front Cover: Shutterstock/Quick Shot; main; Shutterstock: Patryk Kosmider tl, Mark Oleksiy cl, Nacho Such bl, Worlds Wildlife Wonders br; Inside: 1, ©Shutterstock/Gary Yim; 4, ©Thinkstock/Michak Lootwijk; 4-5, ©Shutterstock/Szetei; 6, ©Shutterstock/Dirk Ercken; 6-7, ©PhotoShot/Gail Shumway; 8, ©FLPA/Martin Willis/Minden Pictures; 8-9, ©Dreamstime/John Carnemolla; 10, ©Shutterstock/Janossy Gergely; 10-11, ©Shutterstock/Cuson; 12, ©Shutterstock/Dang Dumrong; 13, ©Shutterstock/Kate Capture; 14, ©Shutterstock/Amskad; 14-15, ©Shutterstock/Jeep2499; 16, ©FLPA/Pete Oxford/Minden Pictures; 17, ©Shutterstock/Bambara; 18, ©Shutterstock/DMV Photos; 18-19, ©Shutterstock/Kjersti Joergensen; 20, ©Shutterstock/Ammit Jack; 21, ©Shutterstock/Mark Oleksiy; 22, ©Shutterstock/Rich Carey; 23, ©Shutterstock/Mikadun.
T=Top, C=Center, B=Bottom, L=Left, R=Right

Brown Bear Books has made every attempt to contact the copyright holder. If you have any information please contact:
licensing@brownbearbooks.co.uk

CONTENTS

Where Do RAIN FORESTS GROW?

Tropical rain forests grow where the weather is hot and very rainy. They grow in countries near the equator. This is the imaginary line that runs around the middle of the Earth.

Leaf cutter ants can carry more than 50 times their own body weight.

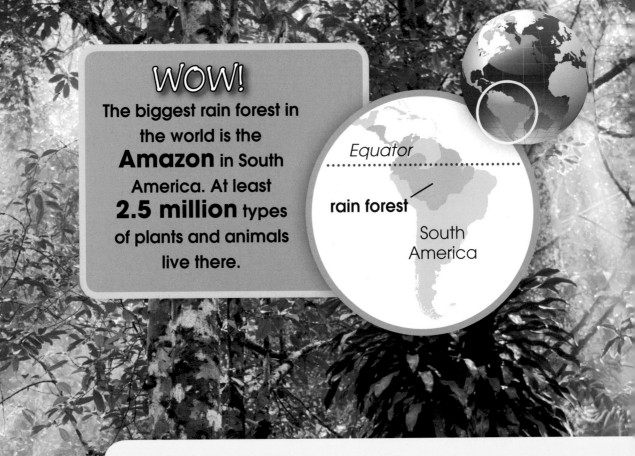

WOW!

The biggest rain forest in the world is the **Amazon** in South America. At least **2.5 million** types of plants and animals live there.

Equator

rain forest

South America

About half of the animals in the world live in rain forests. Many live high in the tree tops because that is where they find their food. You can find out about some rain forest animals in this book.

FROGS

Many different frogs live in rain forests. Some are brightly colored—red, blue, or green. Flying frogs spread out their webbed feet to **glide** between trees.

This is a poison dart frog. It has poison in its skin.

Flying frogs have big pads on their toes that help them stick to trees when they land. They eat insects.

TREE KANGAROO

Tree kangaroos live high in the rain forests of New Guinea and Australia.

A baby is called a joey. When it is born it climbs into its mother's pouch. It lives there for the first months of its life.

These animals have long tails and strong arms. Their curved claws help them climb trees. They can **jump** a **long** way from trees to the ground—up to 60 feet (18 m).

SLOTH

Sloths are slow-moving animals. They spend the days sleeping. They wake up at night and eat leaves, fruit, and buds. Then they go to sleep again.

Sloths often sleep for 10 hours at a time.

Most sloths are the same size as a small dog. Their strong front legs and long claws help them hang from trees.

Baby sloths are born in trees while their mother hangs upside down!

ORANGUTAN

These large orange apes have very **long** arms. They can be 7 feet (2 m) from fingertip to fingertip.

Orangutans make leafy nests to sleep in. They use big leaves as umbrellas.

A mother looks after her baby for six or seven years.

Gibbons can move fast. They speed along at 35 mph (56 kph) and make huge leaps.

GIBBON

Gibbons are the acrobats of the rain forest. They **swing** through the trees, gripping branches with long, strong hands.

JAGUAR

The jaguar is the **biggest** cat in South America. It is a predator. The markings on its coat help it hide among the plants and shadows of the rain forest as it hunts other animals.

The markings on a jaguar's coat are called rosettes.

Jaguars are good swimmers.
They catch and eat fish, turtles,
and small alligators. On land,
they hunt for prey, such as deer.

AYE-AYE

The small aye-aye lives in the rain forests of Madagascar. It sleeps most of the day.

These animals have big ears and thin fingers.

Aye-ayes use their **long** middle finger to hook grubs to eat from under the bark of trees.

A tarsier is smaller than a man's hand.

TARSIER

The tarsier is a tiny animal with **huge** eyes. The eyes help it to hunt at night. It cannot move its eyes, but it can turn its head to face backward.

CHIMPANZEE

Chimpanzees live in big groups in African rain forests. They stand and walk upright, or walk on all fours. They also **swing** through the trees on long arms.

Baby chimps stay with their mother for six years.

Chimps use sticks to dig grubs out of logs to eat. They also smash open nuts with stones. They sleep in nests that they make from leaves and branches.

TAPIR

Tapirs are **big** animals like pigs.
They love water and wallowing in mud.

WOW!
A tapir pulls
fruit and leaves
off trees with
its short,
bendy trunk.

A toucan's beak can be 7.5 inches (19 cm) long.

TOUCAN

Toucans live high in the trees of the Amazon rain forest. They use their **big**, colorful beaks to pick fruit and catch insects to eat.

RAIN FOREST FACTS

 There two types of rain forests. The tropical ones are always hot. Temperate rain forests are cool in winter and hot in summer.

 Rain forests are very wet. Around 78 inches (198 cm) of rain fall on them every year.

 Tropical rain forests can be about 80°F (27°C) in the day and almost as hot at night.

Rain forests are getting smaller. People are cutting them down. They use the wood from the trees and plant crops or build roads on the land.

USEFUL WORDS

equator
The imaginary line around the middle of the Earth. Countries near the equator are very hot.

glide
To move smoothly.

predator
An animal that hunts and kills other animals for food. The jaguar is a predator. →

prey
An animal hunted and eaten by another animal. Deer are the prey of a jaguar.

FIND OUT MORE

Amazon Rainforest
William B. Rice, Time for Kids, 2012

Eyewonder: Rainforest
DK, 2013

Food for Life series, Rainforests Kate Riggs, Creative Education, 2010

Tropical Rainforest Simon Seymour, Smithsonian, 2010.

INDEX